The Best Day Ever!

By Vera Edobor

Illustrations by Nicole Wolf and TJ

The Best Day Ever!
by Vera Edobor
Illustrations by Nicole Wolf and TJ

Printed in the United States of America

ISBN 9781628391176

www.xulonpress.com

Dedication

To our children:

Princess

Ese and Efe

Prince E

Jesus loves you; this I know. Thank you for honoring the LORD!

Hello friend,

I'm so glad you got this book! You are a child of promise and God has sent me to show you just how much He loves and cares for you! This book tells the story of David and how he became Jesus' special friend. You too can become Jesus' special friend and share His love with people around you. Trust me, life is so much easier and better when Jesus is a part of it. 'The Best Day Ever!' is followed by a series of other interesting books including:

- A New Day at School
- Yummy in my Tummy
- What Does God Want From Me?

May you really be blessed as you walk closer to Jesus. Happy reading!

Vera

Once upon a time, there was a little boy whose name was David. He was seven years old and in the first grade. Before he left for school each morning, his mum packed a lunch full of nutritious food, fruits and milk. She always put David's water bottle by the side of his backpack and reminded him to drink his water and milk at school. However, each time David got to school, he was always attracted to the pop cans displayed in the vending machine. The thought of pop filled his heart the whole day and he became very restless.

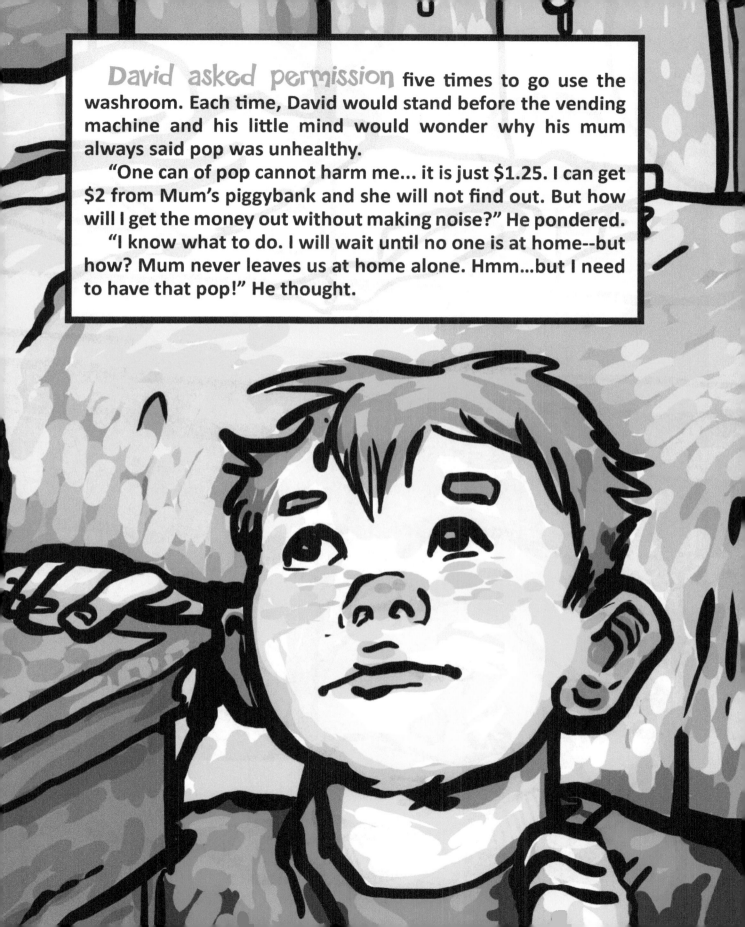

David asked permission five times to go use the washroom. Each time, David would stand before the vending machine and his little mind would wonder why his mum always said pop was unhealthy.

"One can of pop cannot harm me... it is just $1.25. I can get $2 from Mum's piggybank and she will not find out. But how will I get the money out without making noise?" He pondered.

"I know what to do. I will wait until no one is at home--but how? Mum never leaves us at home alone. Hmm...but I need to have that pop!" He thought.

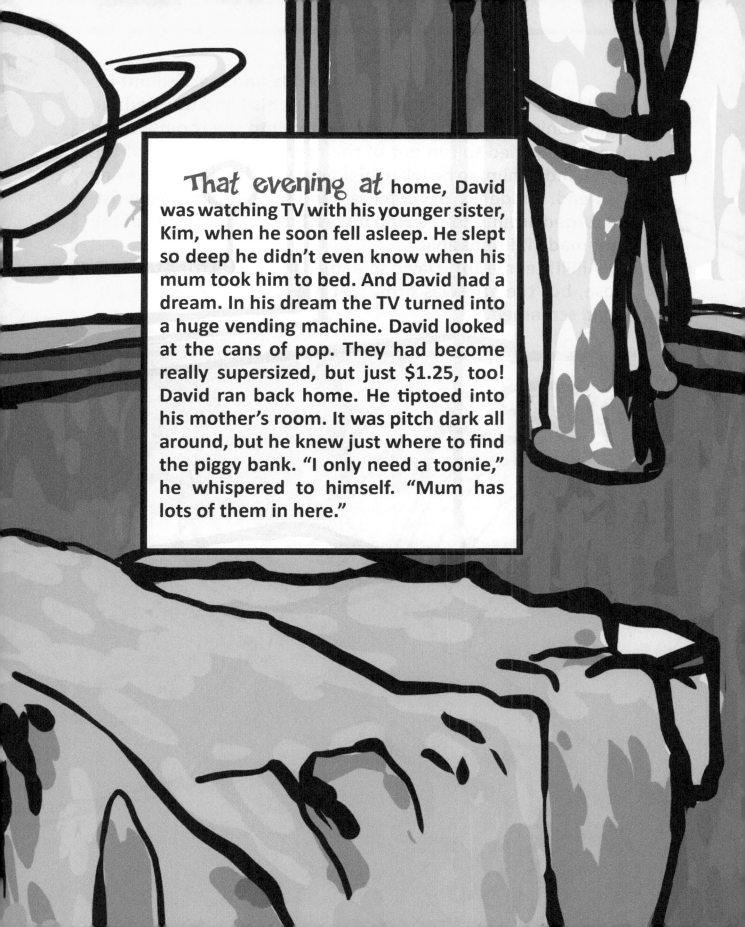

That evening at home, David was watching TV with his younger sister, Kim, when he soon fell asleep. He slept so deep he didn't even know when his mum took him to bed. And David had a dream. In his dream the TV turned into a huge vending machine. David looked at the cans of pop. They had become really supersized, but just $1.25, too! David ran back home. He tiptoed into his mother's room. It was pitch dark all around, but he knew just where to find the piggy bank. "I only need a toonie," he whispered to himself. "Mum has lots of them in here."

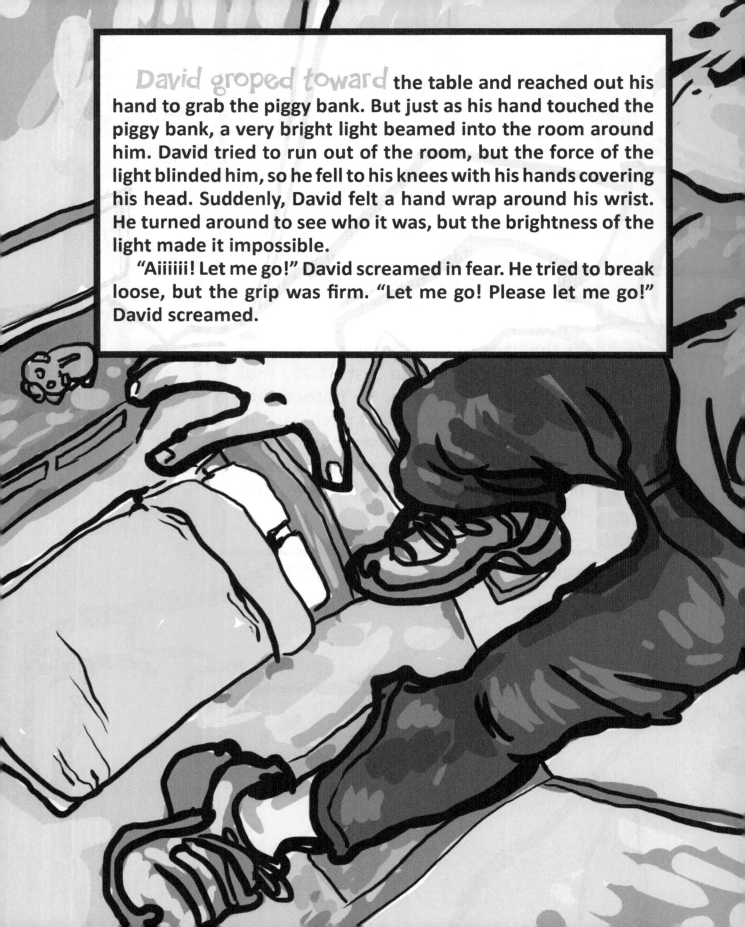

David groped toward the table and reached out his hand to grab the piggy bank. But just as his hand touched the piggy bank, a very bright light beamed into the room around him. David tried to run out of the room, but the force of the light blinded him, so he fell to his knees with his hands covering his head. Suddenly, David felt a hand wrap around his wrist. He turned around to see who it was, but the brightness of the light made it impossible.

"Aiiiiii! Let me go!" David screamed in fear. He tried to break loose, but the grip was firm. "Let me go! Please let me go!" David screamed.

The force from the hand lifted him off his feet and started pulling him toward the source of light. David screamed, "Mummy, Mummy!" but she did not hear him. David sailed through the air, over many rivers, lands, mountains and valleys for what seemed like many years. Finally, the hand set David down in a big wide-open field surrounded by beautiful trees. David landed softly on the green grass. David lifted up his face and saw a man dressed in a flowing robe standing before him. His clothes shone brighter than the dazzling sun.

Suddenly David overflowed with excitement and he brightened up.

"I...know... you," he stammered.

"Yes, David, you know me."

"I...know... you. I've...seen...you... before. You...You look like...Jesus," David said.

"That's right, David, I am Jesus."

"But...but...are you real? I thought you were make believe like Superman ...and Spiderman...and my favorite superhero, Batman!"

"No, David, I am real and you can see me, can't you?" Jesus asked.

"**Yes, I can** see you. But I thought...well...never mind. What are we doing here? Where is this place? Are you going to hurt me?" David asked fearfully. "I only wanted a toonie. Please don't tell my mum! She will be mad at me. She said I couldn't have any pop. P-l-e-a-s-e." He begged.

"No, David, I would never think of hurting you. I brought you here because I am hurting and I am wondering if you could help me with a few things," Jesus said.

"Me? But I am just a kid. You are all grown up. What can I help you with?" David inquired.

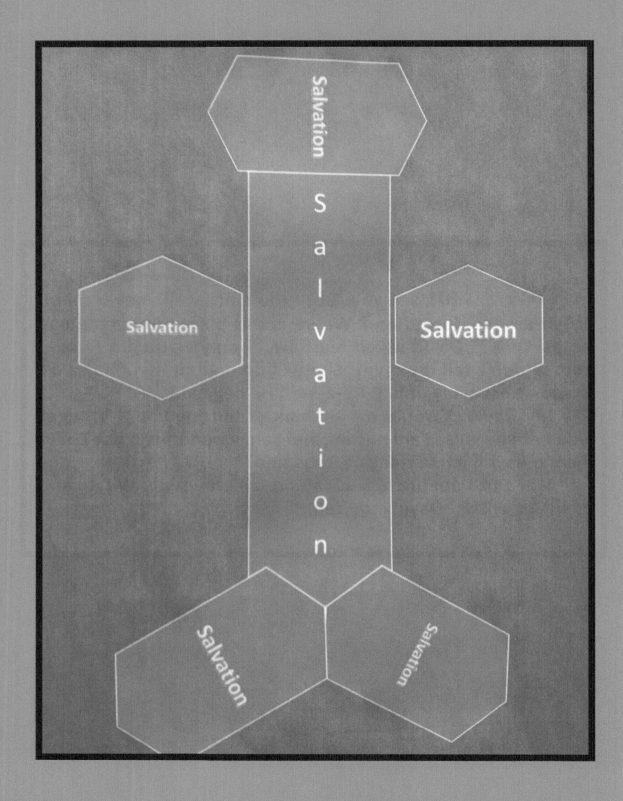

"A lot, David—more than you realize. I know you are a very smart little boy and I would love to share my story with you. Would you like to hear it?" Jesus asked David.

"Yes I would, and I would help you if I could," David responded.

"Thanks, David. I knew I could count on you. Have you ever heard the word *salvation*? Does it mean anything to you?" Jesus asked.

"Salvation? I have heard of it, but I don't know what it really means. Is that what is hurting you? Does it make people sad?" David asked.

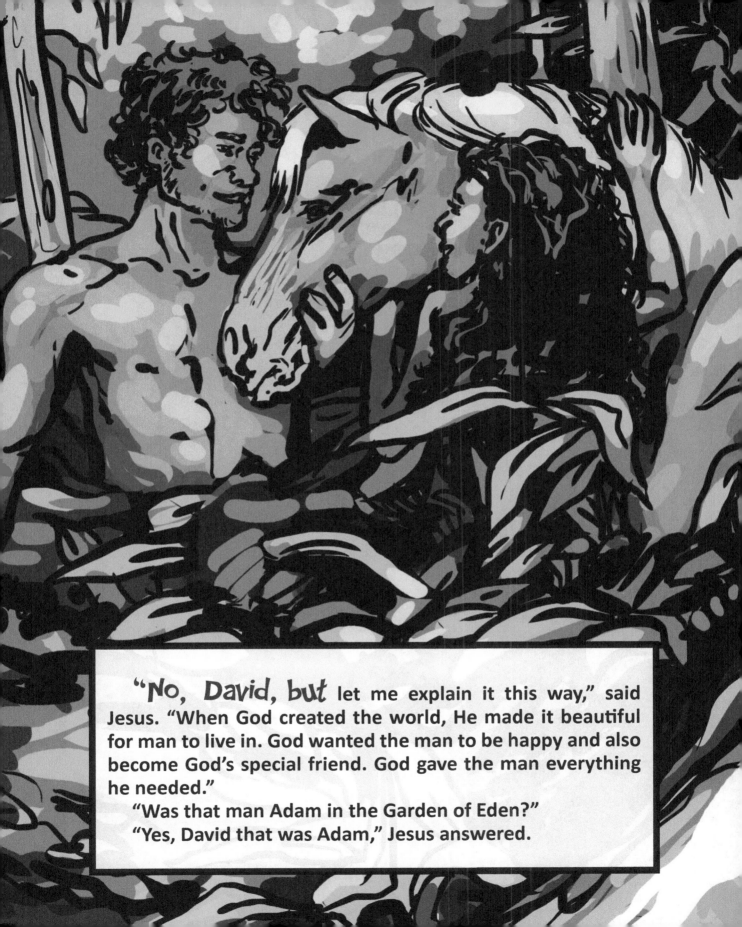

"No, David, but let me explain it this way," said Jesus. "When God created the world, He made it beautiful for man to live in. God wanted the man to be happy and also become God's special friend. God gave the man everything he needed."

"Was that man Adam in the Garden of Eden?"

"Yes, David that was Adam," Jesus answered.

"Our teacher taught us about Adam and Eve at church. I know the story. Satan came and told Eve to eat the forbidden fruit and she did. She disobeyed God and listened to Satan. But is Satan really real? Where is he and how come we don't see him? I know he is really mean." David commented.

"You may not see Satan, David, but he is real," Jesus said.

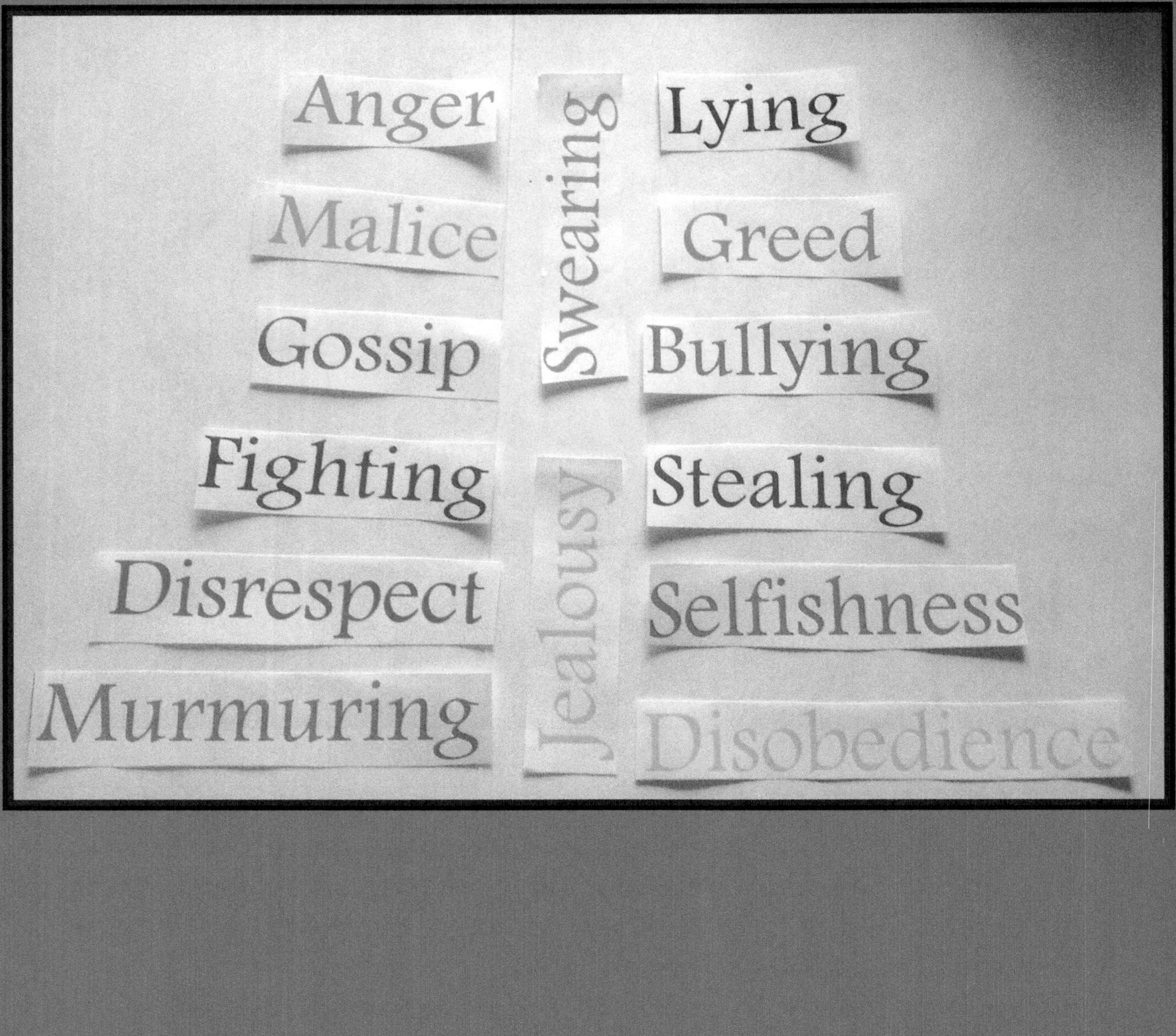

Anger

Malice

Gossip

Fighting

Disrespect

Murmuring

Swearing

Jealousy

Lying

Greed

Bullying

Stealing

Selfishness

Disobedience

"Satan wanted Adam and Eve to disobey God and not be friends with Him anymore. Satan wanted them to be his own servants instead. So when Eve ate the fruit and also shared some with Adam, Satan gained control of their minds. He made Adam and Eve do everything that God said He hated."

"You mean like lying and stealing and disobeying our parents?" David asked Jesus.

"Yes, David and a lot of other evil things which we call sins. God hated sin and still does.

"**Now when Adam** and Eve sinned, how do you think God felt?"
"Sad and angry?"
"Very sad, David. God became very sad and His heart was broken. Adam and Eve became very sad and lonely too because they discovered that Satan deceived them. They saw that Satan was mean, selfish, and really wanted to destroy them. They wanted to become God's friends again, but Satan was now their boss. God also wanted to be man's friend again, but man was now all covered in sin. He was so dirty and filthy that God couldn't even touch him.

And you know what was worse?"

"What?"

"Adam and Eve knew that anyone who sinned would be punished. He would be put in a lake of fire for all eternity."

"That's scary." David said. "Did God want His friend to die and go into the fire? Why didn't God help him?"

"He did," said Jesus. Because God loved man so much, He sent me to come help man clean up Satan's mess."

"And you did? How did you do that?" David asked.

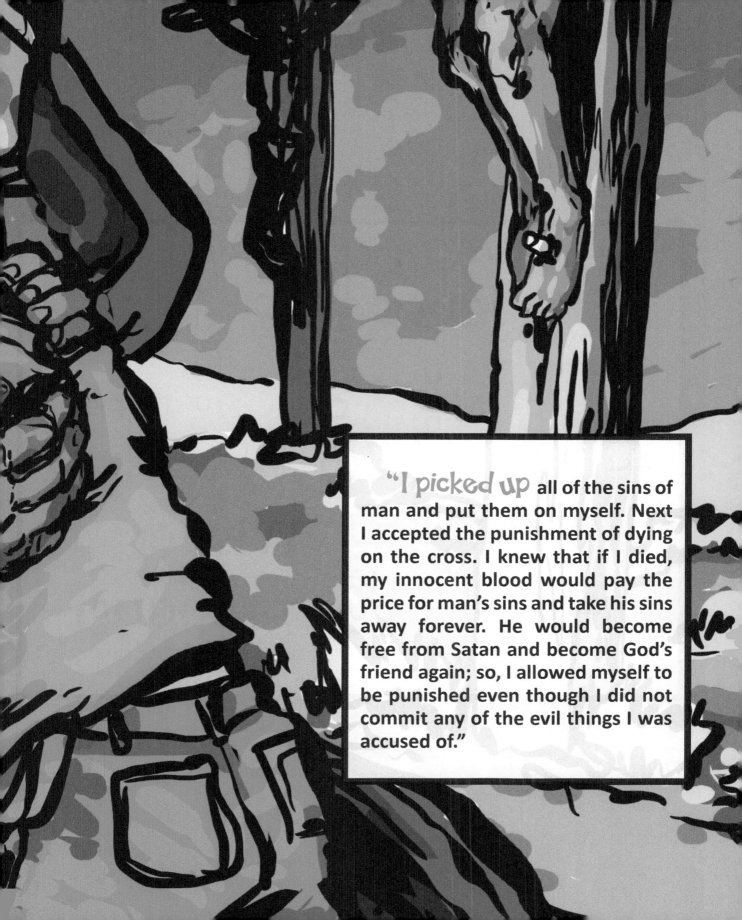

"I picked up all of the sins of man and put them on myself. Next I accepted the punishment of dying on the cross. I knew that if I died, my innocent blood would pay the price for man's sins and take his sins away forever. He would become free from Satan and become God's friend again; so, I allowed myself to be punished even though I did not commit any of the evil things I was accused of."

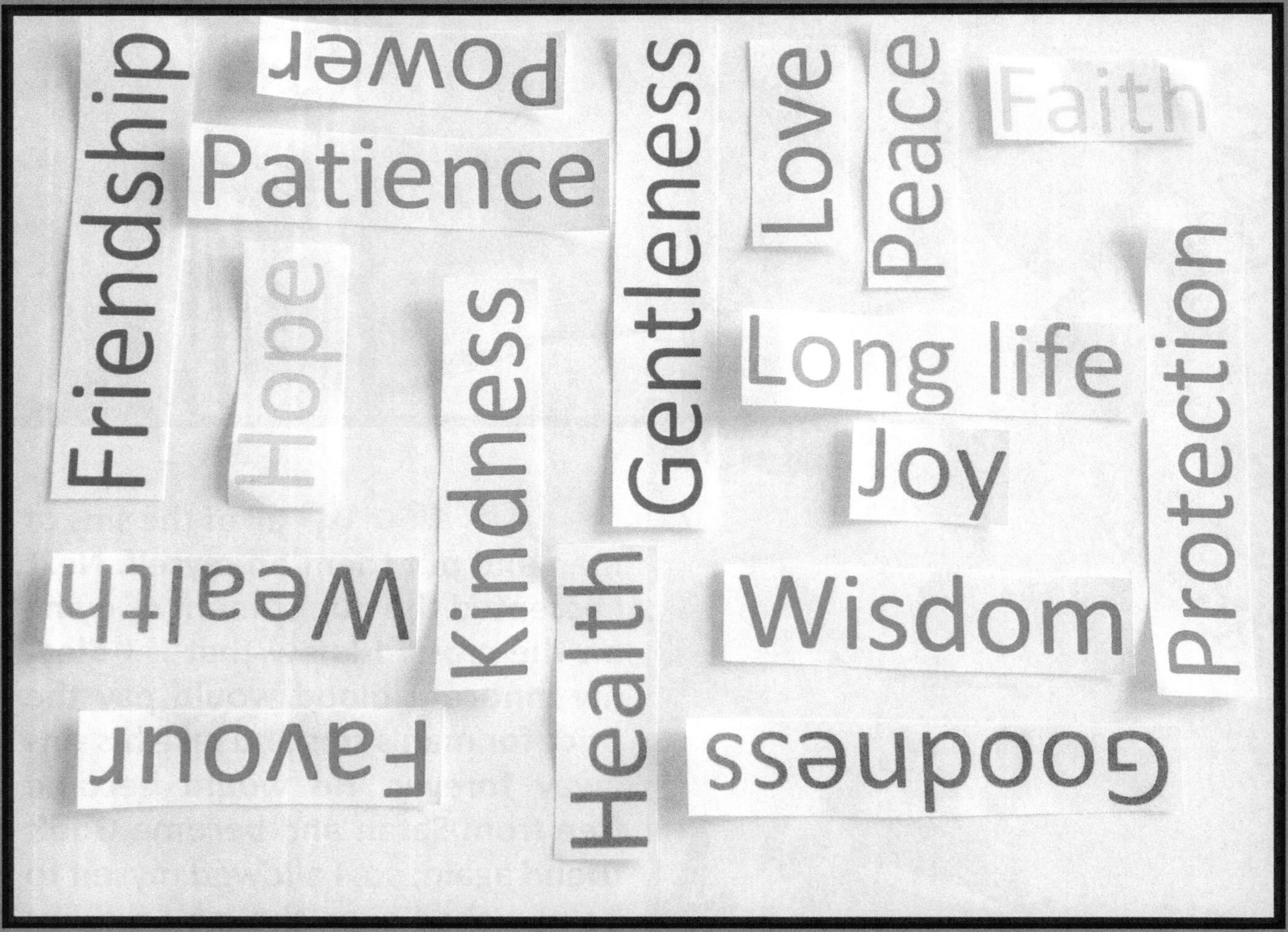
Friendship
Power
Patience
Gentleness
Love
Peace
Faith
Hope
Kindness
Long life
Joy
Protection
Wealth
Health
Wisdom
Favour
Goodness

"Our teacher said you rose again after you died because you are so powerful. He said you are stronger than Satan and you took away his power. Is that true?" David asked.

"That is true, David." Jesus replied. "I also gave man the power to take back all that Satan took from him—health, peace, love and joy. Everything!"

"You did?" David asked.

"Yes David, I did. Anyone who believes in me receives that power and is no longer afraid of Satan. He becomes a brand new man who is fit for my use and then I can make him work in my field."

"Your field? Where is that?" David asked. At that moment, Jesus turned to David and said,

"Lift up your eyes now, David, and tell me what you see."

"I see people ... I see so many different people. Is this your field?"

"Yes, David, but you call it church," replied Jesus.

"I go to church every Sunday with my mum, my dad and my little sister, Kim."

"That's very good, David. The church is where I feed you my word and give you instructions to help keep you away from Satan. Anyone who listens to my word and obeys it becomes my special friend. I give him special gifts. I go with him wherever he goes and I teach him about my kingdom.

"I want to be your special friend, too. Can I have one of your special gifts? David asked Jesus.

"Yes, David. Here you are. This is my very special gift to you. It is the precious gift of salvation. With it, you can withstand any trick of Satan. You and all my other friends can also tell people about me and my kingdom. It also gives you the direction to my kingdom and an invitation for you to come there. So when you grow old and die, you will come and reign with me there."

"**And that is** heaven, isn't it? I really want to go there. Our teacher said there is no place like it in the whole wide world!" David exclaimed.

"Your teacher is right. Heaven is a beautiful place and I promise to bring you there when the time comes—if you'd love to come," Jesus responded.

"**Of course I** would love to! Thank you so much for giving me the gift of salvation and letting me be a part of your kingdom. I will do a lot better at church from now on. I will listen to your word and follow your instructions. I will also ask my sister and all my friends to listen as well. I will let them know that you have special gifts for those who obey you. We will not allow Satan to control our minds or make us disobey you."

"Very well said, David."

"That's not all. I will be a good boy at home, at school, at church and wherever I may be. I will tell people about your love for them, about your kingdom and your special gifts for them if they do the things that you like." David responded.

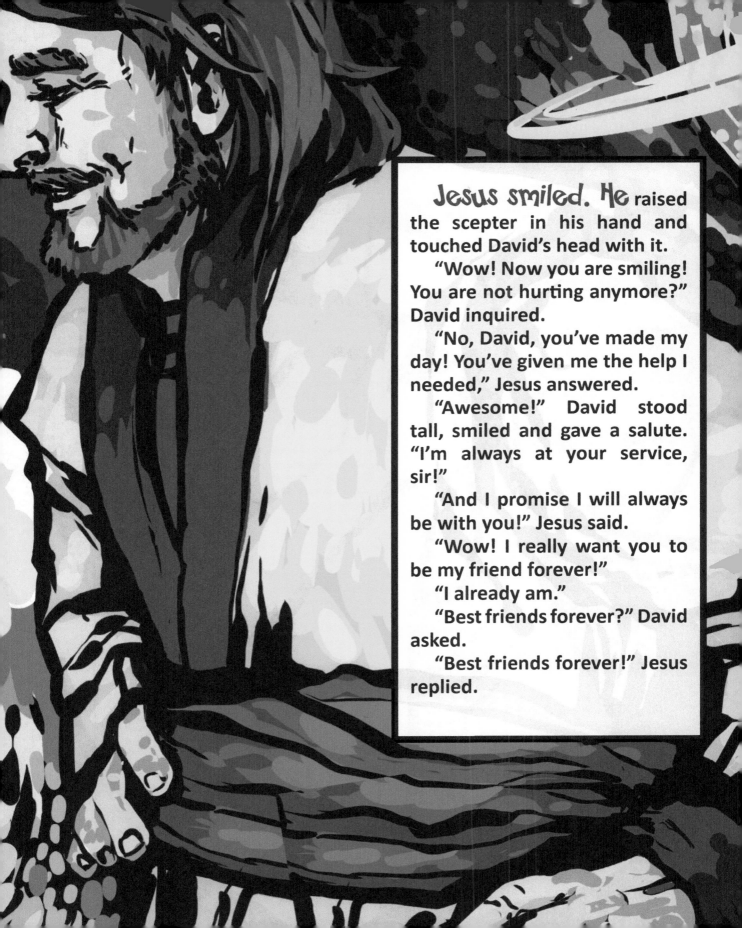

Jesus smiled. He raised the scepter in his hand and touched David's head with it.

"Wow! Now you are smiling! You are not hurting anymore?" David inquired.

"No, David, you've made my day! You've given me the help I needed," Jesus answered.

"Awesome!" David stood tall, smiled and gave a salute. "I'm always at your service, sir!"

"And I promise I will always be with you!" Jesus said.

"Wow! I really want you to be my friend forever!"

"I already am."

"Best friends forever?" David asked.

"Best friends forever!" Jesus replied.

And as David looked, Jesus was lifted up into the beautiful blue sky and soon a huge cloud covered him. David felt so happy.

A few minutes later, David woke up and felt so good. "Yes, this is the best day ever! I am willing to live forever for Jesus!" He said to himself. David grinned as his mum walked into the room. He jumped down from his bed and gave his mum a very big hug.

"Hey David, how come you are up so early and with such a big smile on your face? What are you so excited about this morning?" David's mother asked.

"Mum," said David, "I saw Jesus! I can't wait to get to school today! I have to tell all my friends about Jesus! Mum, I saw Jesus! HE...IS...SO...COOL!"

And as David went off to school that morning, he beamed with a new sense of focus and enthusiasm, remembering the kindness and the words of Jesus. It was going to be a great day, and he knew it!

THE END

CPSIA information can be obtained at www.ICGtesting.com
Printed in the USA
LVOW02s0701150913

352458LV00001B/1/P

9 781628 391176